Marriage Is Work!
Who Told You It
Wasn't?

Benny L. Dozier Sr.

Marriage Is Work! Who Told You It Wasn't?
Copyright © 2012 by Benny L. Dozier, Sr.

ABLE Publications

Bookcover: TS DesignStudio
Artwork: Eric Bruns

ISBN 978-0-9885463-1-8

DEDICATION

First, I want to thank you God for your Spirit, the Holy Spirit, for inspiring me to write this book. I can do nothing that is of any substance without you, Holy Spirit.

I would like to dedicate this book to my little lady- my wife Gerry. I want to thank God for my son Benny Jr., my firstborn, who is doing outstanding work in ministry- Love you, Ben. I want to thank God for my son Darryl, who is doing outstanding work in ministry and is my personal armourbearer, and for my daughter-in-law Chanan (they wrote the foreword for this book) –you all are a great couple, and to my three beautiful granddaughters- I love you, girls. I want to also dedicate this book to all of the couples of Power and Light Ministries and the A.P.I.N. I love you all.

This book is dedicated in loving memory to one of my longtime friends, spiritual son, and elder, Acie McCullough. Elder Acie and his wife Elder Betty were married for 38 years and had a wonderful marriage! We miss Acie but we know he is with God. We love you Elder Betty.

TABLE OF CONTENTS

FOREWORD

This book embodies 37 years of successful marriage. It is filled with truths and realities, no fairytale stories about marriage. If you want to stay married and actually experience success against the odds, this is the book for you and your spouse. This is not a one-time read but a marriage reference guide to be utilized from your wedding day until death do you part. **I know what you are thinking.......Who are we? We are a true testament to the fact that the principles in this book work.**

We are so blessed to have such awesome examples living in our midst. They are not only our spiritual parents but they are also our natural parents. I (Darryl Dozier) had the pleasure of seeing my parents Benny & Geraldine Dozier's (authors of this book) marriage firsthand. While growing up as a child in this family I saw the contents of this book exemplified through their lifestyle. Looking back, I didn't fully grasp the effort or sacrifice that my parents put into developing a healthy marriage until I became married myself. I watched them time after time manage the challenges of working full time jobs, starting a new ministry, finishing school and dealing with the loss of close family members. In the midst of these, their love for one another and for me and my brother was always present. They constantly worked hard to spend quality time with one another and us.

I (Chanan Dozier) met this awesome couple for the first time in 1988 as a member of their church. When Darryl and I got married, I was able to see firsthand that the life they taught about was exactly what they lived. They put effort into having a great marriage. I come from a blended family. I have totally awesome parents and they worked hard to give us the world!! We had a great life, but just in two homes. Because of my upbringing, I had a different belief about marriage. This created a very interesting dynamic in our home once Darryl and I got married.

Without the teachings in this book there is no way our marriage would have made it. Divorce is at an all-time high and I can honestly see why. Many people enter into marriage thinking that things will just work themselves out but that is not true. You have to work your marriage. If you enter into marriage without the tools you need or don't seek Godly counsel you will either stay unfulfilled in your marriage or leave your spouse thinking that it wasn't meant to be, when the truth of the matter is that marriage calls for work. Think of it as a great sweat equity investment that will keep giving back to you.

Regardless of the condition or stage of your marriage (i.e. newlyweds, seasoned, separated, unfulfilled/unhappy) this book will enhance and strengthen it. If you are dealing with unrealistic expectations, identifying blowouts or recognizing inner vows you will see your marriage in the pages of this book. This book is filled with strong practical principals about marriage that have been developed through real life experiences. As you read this book you will discover your own "Ah Hah" moments that will enlighten and bring clarity to your marriage.

10 years and 3 children later, our marriage is thriving because of the wisdom in this book. We were both VIRGINS when we got married! Meaning: No Oral Sex, No Text sex, No Vaginal sex, etc..... ☺ We know what you are thinking now..... How was the honeymoon? It was a wonderful time of exploring! After exploring the sexual aspect of our marriage, our marriage progressed on past the sex and into the phase of two becoming one. We have built businesses together and have individual careers. Our marriage is still progressing but not without sweat equity!

Early on in our marriage, one of the challenges we faced was how to deal with unrealistic expectations of one another. My wife thought that I should already know what to do and when to do it. For instance, Romance.... This is a big one in marriage. She believed I should know what she liked and disliked and that she should not have to tell me. She felt that if she told me it wouldn't flow from my heart. We found out that communicating your desires doesn't take away from your spouse's desire to please you. As the wife, my husband Darryl expected me to handle everything for him like I was his mother. He expected me to cook really well, pay all the bills, work full time, clean everything (when I was a junky person), and be ready for good loving! We both learned that marriage is about leaving and cleaving (Genesis 2:24). It was great for me to want a spouse that had traits like my mom but I had to leave the expectations of what I wanted my wife to be and cleave to the wife God was developing her to be for me. The truth is, marriage is built on open communication and not individual assumptions. So using the wisdom in this book we got to a place where we both communicated what we wanted from each other.

As we progressed further in our marriage we encountered more dynamics that challenged but also enhanced us. It was no longer just us; when you compound marriage, with children, the pressures of individual jobs/careers, up and downs of growing a business and progressing in identifying your God-given assignments in ministry, you can easily become emotionally overwhelmed and lose focus on meeting each other's needs. We began to experience emotional constipation which led to what the book references as "blowouts". We both can attest to being frustrated with each other at times and feeling unheard which caused us not to effectively communicate our true feelings, desires and needs.

When you talk about marriage you are talking about two people becoming one like the book says. But, that includes all of the experiences that have shaped who each person has become. Most of the time when we don't know how to deal with the pain or disappointments we faced in life we make statements to protect ourselves. These statements overflow into our marital relationship and are described by the author as inner vows. He brings so much clarity when dealing with this part of marital relationship. We both can attest to discovering vows that we made throughout our lives which had an impact on our marriage.

Chanan: I know that I came into my marriage with some fears about marriage because my parents divorced, so I started off saying inadvertently, "I will be nice all the time because I want this to work." There is no way to be nice all the time. So when things would come up in our marriage I would try to minimize them until I had the infamous blow-out that is talked about in the book. I didn't know that I had made this inner vow until we received the teachings from this book. After that, I broke the vow using the techniques in the book and have done much better communicating my concerns before I am overwhelmed.

Darryl: Through the revelation of this book I realized that I came into my marriage with a very negative outlook on life. After the teaching in this book I realized that this perception of life came from what is described in this book as bitter expectations. I had experienced some disappointments in life so in response to the pain I didn't want to allow myself to expect the best. So to protect myself I figured if I started off thinking the worse then I wouldn't be disappointed when things didn't work out the way that I planned.   This caused a strained on my marriage and made Chanan feel that I didn't believe in the things we were doing.   Once I got the revelation from this book, I applied it to the inner vow I had made and now I expect the best out of my marriage and life.

Whether you consider your marriage to be great or on its last leg, this book is for you. We can attest to richness and authenticity of the wisdom in this book. If you take this book and put into action the principles that apply to your marriage, there is no way your marriage will stay the same. You will be empowered with the tools you need to build a real and lasting marriage. If you are newly married, this book will carry you through the growing pains as your marriage develops. In marriage there is always room for improvement, so if things are going great they can always get better. Take this guide and use it to take your marriage to the next level. We did and our marriage has never been the same!!

P.S. We are so thankful to be under the tutelage of Benny & Gerry Dozier.

Darryl & Chanan Dozier

PREFACE

*E*very marriage begins with two imperfect people with hopes, dreams and expectations of becoming one. But we have discovered it takes working in concert with God and each other over the life span of the marriage to accomplish this supernatural experience. Sure, it becomes challenging at times to work out difficulties within marriage when you are working with imperfections. But it's worth the sacrifice when you begin to experience the benefits of all your hard work!

*W*ith the help of the Holy Spirit, for over 37 years my husband and I are enjoying the supernatural experience of being "one flesh!" Although we don't have all the answers, we have discovered tools that we desire to pass along from the Word of God that have equipped us over these years, with the help of the Holy Spirit, to remove imperfections that threatened to hinder our marriage in its early tender stages and as it progressed through the years.

*A*fter counseling couples for over twenty-five years, we have discovered that when imperfections are not worked on and removed in the early stages, or as the marriage progresses, they become imbedded within the foundation. The marriage becomes like hardened cement and almost virtually impossible to remove without breaking up the entire foundation.

*W*ith divorce on the rise within the nation, and in the Body of Christ, the Holy Spirit has given us a burning passion for couples to experience the supernatural power of joining and becoming one flesh! (Gen. 2:24)

*O*ur prayer is that as you work with these and other tools you discover in the Word of God, that you too will experience tremendous breakthrough in those challenging areas of your marriage. If you're ready, pick up your tools and go to work! You won't regret it!

Geraldine Dozier
(The Wife and Rib of Benny Dozier)

INTRODUCTION

God in all His sovereignty instituted marriage before He built His church. God is family because in Genesis 1:26 He says, *"Let Us make man in Our image, according to Our likeness;"* God the Father, God the Son, and God the Holy Spirit made man. Marriage plays a significant part in the household of faith (the Church).

God talks about marriage from Genesis to Revelation. He wants us to know His thoughts which are very important to us. God mentions several couples that were given assignments:

Abraham and Sarah (Genesis 12:5)

Issac and Rebekah (Genesis 24:67)

Elkanah and Hannah (I Samuel 1:8)

Zacharias and Elizabeth (Luke 1:5)

Notice how these couples had a reverence for God. All four couples believed in God. The bible talks of how they were married for some time but were all lacking something in their marriage that they couldn't get from each other but had to get from God. Just a side note as you begin to read this book: Don't be afraid of the couples in the bible- We must be able to relate to them if we intend to have the kind of marriages they had in order to get what they got from God.

I began to study another couple in the bible- Aquila and Priscilla. Aquila and Priscilla, were an awesome couple (the Apostle Paul's 'companion couple') who served him diligently. I wanted to know what made their relationship as husband and wife so supernatural. There was such balance – being able to keep their focus on God and the work that they were helping Apostle Paul do, while at the same time enjoying each other as though they had just met for the first time. Can you imagine this awesome couple-having their own tent business, and being a preaching team capable of teaching a great man of God such as Apollos. I was totally intrigued by this couple and I began to think about my relationship with my lovely wife Gerry. Throughout the thirty-seven years of being married, God has given me revelation knowledge based on the bible, the same kind of wisdom and knowledge that He had given Aquila and Priscilla. Then God began to show me that my wife and I were a couple similar to the ones we see in the scripture.

You can only get so much from each other and then you're going to run out of patience, endurance, strength, joy, and tolerance because we are all mere human beings. What these couples were lacking they couldn't get it from anyone but God. Once they believed and accepted that fact, their marriage went to another level. Until you accept the fact that your entire marriage is not totally based upon what you can give to each other, but it's based upon what God can give to each of you and what each of you can give to each other, then your marriage won't be fulfilling.

You cannot have a marriage that excludes God and His purpose for marriage. We must be able to distinguish between a man-made assignment that has been attached to a marriage versus a marriage with a God-given assignment. A marriage with a man-made assignment can only go as far as man can go. When there's a problem it can only think as far as man can think, which has limitations. It must be driven by human beings and humans get tired, quit, and give up. In a marriage with a God-given purpose, when problems arise we can go to and consult God because He's not limited in His answers and solutions. As humans we will get tired, but if that marriage is made by God, even when you are tired or thinking about stopping or giving up, God is obligated to help you since He's the one that made it.

God's plan for us is that marriage is not for a season or time, but for life.

So how do you build a healthy and sound marriage? Begin by implementing and applying these things:

1. You start off with God, the husband, and wife;
2. Let God show you the purpose for your marriage;
3. Both spouses should have an open heart and an open mind;

4. Both spouses must have a desire to forgive and forget;

5. You and your spouse must have a willingness to compromise;

6. The two of you must have a desire to trust;

7. Both spouses must have a willingness to wait;

8. The husband and wife must ask God to give them both a high level of tolerance.

I have a passion for marriage. I have been married to Gerry for 37 years, which has helped me be who I am today. Marriage gives you an opportunity to have a true friend. Marriage is powerful because it has the anointing of God's Spirit upon it. God said, *"Therefore a man shall leave his father and mother and be joined to his wife, and they shall become one flesh" (Genesis 2:24).* A married couple has the anointing of God on their lives. I believe that a husband that loves God has an anointing to carry out that role for God's glory, and the wife has the same anointing as well. I must say that I really love being married and am thankful for my marriage. This book will bless any couple of any ethnic group, any income level, no matter what career you may have, or if you have children or not, or if you are facing some serious challenges in your life or things are going quite well.

If you are reading this book I'm sure that you do not want to be married and living in the same house with your spouse and the marriage is dead. What causes a marriage to die is when it stops producing life. What produces life in a marriage is when God breathes purpose into the marriage- when God breathes into a marriage it becomes alive.

I am pleased to give you what God has given to us in our process of being made into the couple we have become. May the time and tools you invest into your own marriage bring you and your spouse great dividends.

Prayer:

Our Father, I worship you in the name of Jesus. I pray that this book will help my marriage. I pray that as a couple we will implement what we have read and learned from this book. In Jesus' name. Amen.

1

Marriage Is Work! Who Told You It Wasn't?

What is a marriage? It is a covenant relationship between a male and female that God has approved with the consummation of sexual intercourse.

"The Pharisees also came to Him, testing Him, and saying to Him, "Is it lawful for a man to divorce his wife for just any reason?" And He answered and said to them, "Have you not read that He who made them at the beginning 'made them male and female,' and said, 'For this reason a man shall leave his father and mother and be joined to his wife, and the two shall become one flesh'? So then, they are no longer two but one flesh. Therefore what God has joined together, let not man separate." They said to Him, "Why then did Moses command to give a certificate of divorce, and to put her away? "He said to them, "Moses, <u>because of the hardness of your hearts,</u> permitted you to divorce your wives, but from the beginning it was not so" (Matthew 19:3-8).

Couples Should Stand On The Covenant That They Have Made With Each Other And With God.

A covenant is stronger than a contract. A contract is based upon what is written on paper. A covenant is based upon what is written in the heart (love). God wants us to be willing and obedient. Obedience without being willing will not work and it won't build a good relationship. God backs up the covenant of marriage. God stands as a witness to marriage, sealing it with the strongest possible word, 'covenant'. 'Covenant' speaks of faithfulness and enduring commitment. God backs up our marriage- His power and authority stands against every enemy that would violently threaten it from without or within.

Divorce is not an option. *"For the Lord God of Israel says that he hates divorce"* (Malachi 2:16a). I believe marriage is until death separates spouses. We do realize that there are some exceptions when divorce does become an option that can be seen in God's word. I believe the reason why so many divorces are taking place within the Church and world is because no one wants to work on their marriage. A marriage is a work in progress. There is no such thing as an overnight successful marriage; a marriage starts off with, 'I don't know what I don't know'.

Do Not Take The Word 'Work' Out Of Your Marriage

You must work to keep your marriage healthy and solid. The devil comes to steal, kill, and destroy (John 10:10). He hates what God has created, instituted, and joined. This includes traditional marriages (marriage between a man and woman) and children. If you see your marriage as a work in progress that God is doing with you and your spouse, you can agree with the words of Bishop T.D. Jakes, "You don't marry perfection, you marry potential." The Hebrew root word for both 'son' and 'daughter' is 'banah', which means, 'to build'. Therefore, the role of the husband and wife are equally important- we simply build in different ways. The key factor is to know that you are building your marriage relationship and to do it together. Both spouses must be willing to build a Godly wall of righteousness around their marriage that will protect them when the evil one comes. *"The righteousness of the upright will deliver them.."* (Proverbs 11:6a; Romans13:12).

> *If you think the person you married could be better, then it's time for you to improve yourself.*

You need God to help you build anything of any value- surely we need Him if we intend to build great marriages! If God isn't a vital part of your marriage, it can easily fail.

When it comes to our spouses we always attract who we are and not who we need. When you marry who you are, both spouses will seek for fulfillment in the same areas from each other- the question is, who will help who first, or will both spouses be willing to help each other at the same time? When we marry our spouses, the choice we make is not determined by what we want but by who we are.

Spouses knowing their role is a key component to helping a couple's marriage be successful. That marriage must be in proper alignment- Christ first, the husband second, and then the wife (Genesis 2:24; I Corinthians 11:3; Ephesians 5:23). Wives, don't stop reading this book! When the bible talks about the husband being the head, it's not referring to control, force, verbal or physical abuse. God does all things decently and in order. The husband is the head of the wife and not the wife the head of the husband (Ephesians 5:23).

Headship Is Divine Order

Headship is divine Order. Headship is what causes the kingdom of God to prosper in every area. Headship establishes vision, purpose and destiny. Headship produces by-products such as joy, peace, kindness, financial stability, stable children, healthy marriages, peaceful evenings and mornings, etc.

Headship is how the anointing (blessings, vision, order) flows from God, down and not up:

"Behold, how good and how pleasant it is for brethren to dwell together in unity! It is like the precious ointment upon the head, that ran down upon the beard, even Aaron's beard: that went down to the skirts of his garments: As the dew of Hermon, and as the dew that descended upon the mountain of Zion: for the Lord commanded the blessings, even life for evermore"
(Psalms 133).

You need a *head* in order to get a*head*!

*"But I would have you know that the **head** of every man is Christ and the **head** of every woman is the man; and the **head** of Christ is God."*
(I Corinthians 11:3)

What happens when there's no divine headship (God's Rule) in a family? The devil will come in and conquer that man's household and the man will not be able to stop him. He might not even realize what he is allowing the devil to do.

"When a strong man armed keepeth his palace, his goods are in peace: But when a stronger than he shall come upon him, and overcome him, he taketh from him all his armour wherein he trusted, and divideth his spoils"
(Luke 11:21-22).

The devil will take his spoil. What is spoil? Wife, children, wealth, inventions, degrees, businesses, land, eternal life and sound, safe love making.

> **Each spouse knowing their role is a key component in your marriage being successful.**

Being *'a husband'* is different than being **the head'** of the home and wife. Being a *'wife'* is different than being a *'helper or helpmeet'*. Webster dictionary defines 'husband' as *'master of a house'*. The Greek word for husband is 'kephale' (kef-al-ay) and means *'head'*. Head-means *'director'* or *'leader'* Wife in the Hebrew is 'ishshah' (ish-shaw) and means *'woman, wife, opposite of man'*. Helper (help meet) in the Hebrew is 'êzer' (ay-zer) and means *'aid or help'*.

The husband must establish authority in his home by recognizing that he must come under authority- that authority is Jesus Christ. The word 'hus-**band**' can be looked at as the one who puts a *'band'* around his home, creating an environment of safety and protection.

The wife being the helper or 'help meet', in being submissive to her husband, doesn't mean that she has no voice, or can't think for herself, or can't help him make right decisions, but it does mean she trusts and loves him enough and believes in him, knowing the decisions he is making will be very beneficial for both of them (Ephesians 5:22).

I encourage both spouses to make a mutual commitment to walk together, with that husband learning to follow Christ while the wife follows her husband.

Practical Tips On Walking Together:

1. Be patient with each other.
2. Communicate with each other.
3. Respect each other.

The Power Of Submission: Not By Force But By Choice

Let's take a moment to look at Eve. Eve chose not to submit to what God had told them and it cost them their home. She took the forbidden fruit because she wanted it, not because Adam asked for it. Why did Eve continue to talk to satan about what she wanted and desired? Because she failed to operate in the power of submission. She had to choose to operate in the spirit of submission. Her husband could not force her to do it (Genesis 3:1-7). The same is with all wives- each must choose to operate in the power of submission. *"Wives, submit to your own husbands as to the Lord"* (Ephesians 5:22). A wife should never fear being led by her husband if they are already being led by God. The power of submission is this: who am I serving- man or God? *"And whatever you do, do it heartily, as to the Lord and not to men..." (Colossians 3:23).* If you make your husband JESUS, then your husband's ways, reactions, attitudes, and neglect will control you and you will serve those things instead of serving the REAL JESUS! Submission is not surrender, withdrawal or apathy. IT DOES NOT MEAN INFERIORITY. It is MUTUAL commitment and cooperation between that husband and wife.

The marriage must be in proper alignment:

CHRIST $\implies$ THE HUSBAND $\implies$ THE WIFE. When the proper authority is established then there will be order and the home will function and blessings will flow.

AUTHORITY $\implies$ ORDER $\implies$ BLESSINGS

> *Submission is mutual commitment and cooperation between the husband and wife.*

LET'S LOOK AT THE WHEEL ALIGNMENT OF A CAR AS AN EXAMPLE OF ALIGNMENT IN MARRIAGE:

When the marriage is **out of alignment** sometimes the couple will **'toe in'**- isolate themselves from the help they need or one spouse will seek for help and the other spouse does not want it. *"A man who isolates himself seeks his own desire; he rages against all wise judgment"* *(Proverbs 18:1).*

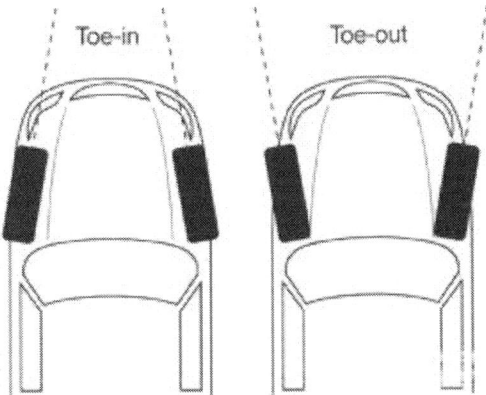

Toe-in   Toe-out

When the marriage is **out of alignment** sometimes the couple will **'toe out'**- both or one spouse will go to a person that is not healthy for their marriage (Proverbs 6:20-29).

THE DOORS ARE OUT OF ALIGNMENT AND CAN'T CLOSE PROPERLY

THERE IS NO CLOSURE UNLESS THE MARRIAGE IS IN PROPER ALIGNMENT.

It becomes difficult to bring closure to disagreements, arguments, mistakes, and the past if your marriage isn't in proper alignment. It becomes difficult to receive inner healing and to retain the healing that comes from breaking inner vows if your marriage is not properly aligned.

When a marriage is in ALIGNMENT the couple becomes a *purpose-driven couple*- a couple that knows their purpose for life individually and corporately (Acts 18:1-3). The wife enjoys the protection and safety that the husband (her head) provides. The husband enjoys the gentle and quiet spirit and words of affirmation that the wife (his helper) provides. To keep your marriage and home in proper alignment you and your spouse must stay open to God, stay open to each other, and stay open to Godly advice.

As the head of your wife, your leadership is influence and the influence you have is produced by a good relationship. The one who has the most influence is the leader of your home (I Timothy 3:4). To rule your home, which is to lead your home is the beginning of leadership- Leadership 101, shall we say. The example you are as the leader of your home is stronger than words. You must know what direction your home is going in and you can't do it by leading from the outside. You must lead from the inside and provide the needed direction for your family.

Every husband that is the head of his home must be prophetic. *'Prophetic'* means God revealing His heart, mind, and thoughts to us. It deals with knowing what God is saying at any given time for you, your life, household, marriage, children, etc. The husband must be able to hear from God in order lead himself and his wife into their God-given purpose. To know God's voice is to know God. To know God is to spend time with Him and in His word.

Three practical ways of hearing God's voice:

1. Spend quiet time listening for God to speak to you.
2. Listen for His voice through dreams and visions.
3. Listen for His voice by reading His word.

The wife can never fully help the husband until the husband fully becomes her head. What causes the wife to become frustrated, feeling empty, inadequate, or not fulfilling the purpose for which she was born is when the husband is not being the head of her life. The husband will feel insecure, unsupported, and will become more vulnerable to negative sources because of the wife not fulfilling her role as his helper.

What are some practical things to do to stay open to God and each other?

1. Pray together daily.

2. Speak life to each other daily.

3. Listen to God's word together regularly.

Is the church perfect? No! Does the Church have problems? Yes! What does Jesus do with a church that has problems? He gives the church an assignment (Matthew 28:19). When Jesus finished communicating to the Church He told the Church, "I will never leave you..." (Matthew 28:20). This declaration was so awesome that it empowered the Church (Acts 1:8, 2:1-4). We, as husbands, have the power to EMPOWER OUR WIVES if we understand our role as the head of our wife and are capable of communicating with her.

What did Jesus keep telling the Church (his wife)? I am going to die but don't worry because when I die, I will be empowered to empower you –The Church, His wife (bride). (John 12:24). The Church didn't fully understand it totally until He died and got up with all power (John 20:19-23). As husbands, our wives will not totally understand until WE DIE AND RECEIVE MORE POWER FROM GOD (grace), humility, humbling ourselves under the mighty hand of God.

How do we die as husbands? First, we must start with answering all these questions:

1. Does your wife have problems?
2. Do you want your wife to understand you more?
3. Do you want your wife to listen to you more?
4. Do you want your wife to be submissive by choice more?
5. Does your wife talk too much?
6. Do you want your wife to stop talking about your marriage to others?
7. Do you sometimes feel that you got married too soon?
8. Don't stop now- were all of your answers 'yes'?
9. If all of your answers were 'yes' *then you have not died yet.*

Notes And Nuggets I Can Use For My Marriage And Personal Development:

2

A Couple's Divine Assignment From God

Give your life to God and He will give you an assignment that will last all of your life- this includes your marriage.
God wants you and your spouse to have a purpose-driven marriage. This is a marriage that has an assignment from God and that assignment becomes the purpose for which you are married.

The assignment God gave Adam and Eve didn't hurt or kill their marriage- it was the lack of carrying out their God-given assignment that hurt their marriage. It opened the door for satan to come in. Anything that has no purpose is destined to die. The word of God tells us, *"Where there is not vision, the people perish" (Proverbs 29:18).*

Marriage Has A Divine Purpose (Genesis 1:28)

All marriages have a divine purpose. I believe that has been one of the most vital elements that caused my marriage to be successful. God gave my wife and I a divine purpose for our marriage and we would seek God for wisdom and revelation on what to do. It gave us focus, excitement, and purpose.

Whatever God joins together in holy matrimony has a divine purpose. (Genesis 2:24) You may say "my marriage is not working!" You must give your marriage something to do. A marriage needs something to do that is God-given and driven by a divine purpose.

You may say "my marriage is so hard to deal with!" You should stop placing bricks in your marriage and start putting cotton in your marriage. Bricks are anger, unforgiveness and selfishness. Cotton is prayer, love, the Word of God, commitment, laughter, humility, good communication, and sex. You may say "I don't understand my marriage!" You have too many heads in your marriage. Take away all the heads and leave one. This means there are too many thoughts, opinions, and ideas that don't lead to the one vision and purpose that God is saying is for your marriage.

> *Anything that has no purpose is destined to die.*

God wants you to be led by His Spirit and the devil wants you to be driven. God wants to reach you as a couple before the devil does. The devil is trying to reach you and get you locked into the cares of this world.

"If anyone comes to me and does not hate his father and mother, wife and children, brothers and sisters, yes, and his own life also, he cannot be my disciple....... So likewise, whoever of you does not forsake all that he has cannot be my disciple"
(Luke 14:26, 33).

"And everyone who has left houses or brothers or sisters or father or mother or wife or children or lands, for My name's sake, shall receive a hundredfold, and inherit eternal life"
(Matthew 19:29).

God wants to reach you and get you locked into His kingdom (doing things God's way) and the cares of this world will be in their right perspective.

But seek ye first the kingdom of God, and his righteousness; and all these things shall be added unto you" (Matthew 6:33).

A couple's divine assignment is when two individual assignments become one assignment by marriage. This becomes **a joint assignment**.

Therefore shall a man leave his father and his mother, and shall cleave unto his wife: and they shall be one flesh" (Genesis 2:24).

Adam had an assignment before he married Eve and Eve had an assignment before she married Adam. Adam's assignment was to dress and keep the Garden of Eden, while Eve's assignment was to be Adam's helpmeet:

"Then God blessed them, and God said to them, "Be fruitful and multiply; fill the earth and subdue it; have dominion over the fish of the sea, over the birds of the

air, and over every living thing that moves on the earth"
(Genesis 1:28).

Do not place the natural man into a divine assignment. Abraham and Sarah placed the natural man into a God-given assignment.

" So Sarai said to Abram, "See now, the LORD has restrained me from bearing children. Please, go in to my maid; perhaps I shall obtain children by her." And Abram heeded the voice of Sarai" (Genesis 16:2).

Whenever your God-given assignment has been cluttered with the thought of the natural man, the devil will capitalize on the confusion that the spouses are going to encounter.

"Then Sarai said to Abram, "My wrong be upon you! I gave my maid into your embrace; and when she saw that she had conceived, I became despised in her eyes. The LORD judge between you and me. So Abram said to Sarai, Indeed your maid is in your hand; do to her as you please." And when Sarai dealt harshly with her, she fled from her presence" (Genesis 16:5-6).

"But the natural man does not receive the things of the Spirit of God, for they are foolishness to him; nor can he know them, because they are spiritually discerned" (I Corinthians 2:14).

When spouses are led by their God-given assignments, the enemy could never run them over or overtake them in any area of their lives.

"For Sarah conceived, and bare Abraham a son in his old age, at the set time of which God had spoken to him." And Abraham was an hundred years old, when his son Isaac was born unto him" (Genesis 21:2, 5).

When a marriage is having severe problems they've left their God-given assignment: A God-given assignment will always keep you focused.

"Looking unto Jesus the author and finisher of our faith; who for the joy that was set before him endured the cross, despising the shame, and is set down at the right hand of the throne of God" (Hebrews 12:2).

Two will never be a marriage until the two become one! (Matthew 19:5-6) A God-given purpose is what joins a husband and a wife.

Prayer for God's Leading
Father in the name of your son Jesus we worship you. Through the blood of Jesus we worship you. We seek you for your leadership, we need you Father to lead us through your Spirit. We won't go unless you lead us. We will wait for your leading. In Jesus' name, Amen.

Notes And Nuggets I Can Use For My Marriage And Personal Development:

3

The Art Of A Relationship Is Communication

Nothing comes easy in a God-given relationship. You must *worship, work and fight* in order to keep a God-given relationship. Healthy communication is key to a successful marriage. If you improve your communication, your relationship will automatically be improved. Master communication and you will manage the conflict.

"Indeed we all make many mistakes. For if we could control our tongues, we would be perfect and could also control ourselves in every other way"
(James 3:2NLT).

Most conflicts that take place in a marriage that become uncontrollable are the result of faulty communication. You may be a good speaker but are you a good communicator?

Faulty Communication

A bad relationship is a sign of faulty communication. In Genesis chapter 3 we see that Adam failed to communicate effectively with his wife. Adam allowed Eve's voice to influence him more than God's voice (Genesis 3:6). Husband, what has God told you to do? What did God tell Adam to do? For every husband that is truly saved, God has and will give them an assignment that will keep the enemy from destroying their marriage. The husband must communicate the assignment to his wife. As a husband you may be asking, 'what assignment?' If so, then I challenge you to communicate with your God- is it faulty or healthy communication?

It's important that the God-given plans, vision, goals, and even what God is doing personally with that husband be communicated effectively to the wife in a way that she will be able to receive it and feel secure and safe enough to follow that husband as he follows Christ (Ephesians 5:21-33).

Poor communication is communication that is built on dishonesty, the absence of a listening ear, and a lot of assumptions. Poor communication is saying what you want someone to hear. Poor communication is hearing what you want to hear. Poor communication is when your tongue is out of timing.

Then his wife said to him, "Do you still hold fast to your integrity? Curse God and die!" But he said to her, "You speak as one of the foolish women speaks. Shall we indeed accept good from God, and shall we not accept adversity?" In all this Job did not sin with his lips"
(Job 2:9-10).

"And it came to pass on the way, at the encampment, that the LORD met him and sought to kill him. Then Zipporah took a sharp stone and cut off the foreskin of her son and cast it at Moses feet, and said, "Surely you are a husband of blood to me!" So He let him go. Then she said, "You are a husband of blood!"—because of the circumcision"
(Exodus 4: 24-26).

"But a certain man named Ananias, with Sapphira his wife, sold a possession, and kept back part of the price, his wife also being privy to it, and brought a certain part, and laid it at the apostles' feet"
(Acts 5:1-2).

Stop 'listening' to your spouse and begin to 'hear' your spouse. Ask God to give you an ear to hear your spouse. *"He that hath an ear let him hear..." (Revelation 2:29).* Going to bed angry can affect the communication in your marriage also. *"In your anger do not sin": Do not let the sun go down while you are still angry, and do not give the devil a foothold" (Ephesians 4:26-27NIV).*

The Power Of A Wife's Words- Your Submission Will Work Every time!

Wives, your words can and do affect your husband.

"If you are a wife, you must put your husband first. Even if he opposes our message, you will win him over by what you do. No one else will have to say anything to him, because he will see how you honor God and live a pure life" (I Peter 3:1-2CEV).

You can affect how your husband manages your home if he doesn't like being there. He sets the tone (the mood and quality) of the home but the wife, with nagging words, can cause that husband to want to dwell in the corner of the housetop or the right words can cause him to want to dwell within the home.

"It's better to stay outside on the roof of your house than to live inside with a   nagging wife"
(Proverbs 21:9CEV).

"It is better to dwell in a desert land than with a contentious woman and with vexation"
(Proverbs 21:19 AMP).

A wife's nagging can cause the enemy to tempt her husband with the thought that there is someplace or someone better than he has at home because of what he is experiencing in his home. It can cause him to think he is losing the ability to run his house and love his wife. This is where the husband must know his role of dying to the flesh and surrendering to Jesus all the more to cause his home to experience healthy living.

"The steady dripping of rain and the nagging of a wife are one and the same. It's easier to catch the wind or hold olive oil in your hand than to stop a nagging wife" (Proverbs 27:15-16CEV).

As a wife, your words have something to do with your level of submission (I Peter 3:1; Ephesians 5:22). According to II Kings 5:1-5, the words of Naaman's wife helped bring healing and deliverance to her husband. Even though Naaman was wrestling with pride, her words were able to get a word to the prophet on her husband's behalf which resulted in his healing and deliverance. The Shunamite woman, with her words and submission, was able to speak to her husband with this profound statement: *"Look now, I know that this is a holy man of God who passeth by us regularly."* Her husband was in agreement and with that mutual agreement they were able to birth a son that they always wanted and release blessings into their home (II Kings 4:1-17). Abigail's words to David literally saved her husband's life and their household (I Samuel 25:1-42). Ladies, the combination of the right words and the spirit of submission can help your marriage. *"Kind words are like honey— they cheer you up and make you feel strong" (Proverbs 16:24CEV)*. Those soft, kind words can cause you to really have your husband's ear.

Where Sex Can't Move Your Husband, Your Soft Words Can

A harlot will use the power of her body to move a man but a mature and wise wife will use the power of her words to move her husband (Proverbs 6:25-26).

Move him with the softness of your words. *"A soft answer turns away wrath, but grievous words stir up anger" (Proverbs 15:1AMP; I Peter 3:1AMP)*. Never attack your husband because of what he is lacking or is in need of. Use the power of your words to establish an altar of prayer in your home. Hanna was battling with some internal problems but she didn't blame her husband. She began to talk to God. By talking and crying out to the Lord she was able to move her husband. The scriptures don't state what Hannah may have said to her husband, but I believe that her words were soft as a result of being in the presence of God and allowing Him to give her the wisdom needed to discuss this challenging situation with her spouse in a way that wouldn't cause wrath or stir up anger (I Samuel 1:8, 15). By the same token, there are times when that wife will be faced with great challenges that may cause an emotional state of great distress as we see with Rachel in Genesis 30:1-2. Usually angry outbursts from that wife toward the husband, will cause an angry response to be reciprocated, as we can see in the case with Jacob and Rachel.

In the 18th chapter of the book of Acts we see where Aquila was able to lead his house into its destiny. This had a lot to do with the fact that he was able to master the skill of hearing (Acts 18:3-4).He was able to hear the Holy Spirit give him directions and heard God through the teaching Paul gave in the church. As a husband, if you can't communicate, you can't lead very well. What hurts or hinders your communication skills is your ability to hear and receive. A great desire to receive builds up your ability to hear. A great ability to hear builds the steps to being able to communicate. If you have great communication going then you're bound to build a great relationship between you and your wife. Being the head of your home and having a great relationship will cause you to become an even greater leader within your home.

How Can I Improve My Relationship With My Spouse?

There are certain statements spouses should remove or keep out of their marriage:

(The Husband saying:) "You're nothing!; "I don't want you!" or "I don't need you!"

(The Wife saying:) "Why don't you be a man!" or "You're not a man!"

"Shoulda, coulda…"

"If I could turn back the hand of time…."

"You never…." (negatively)

"You always…." (negatively)

> **If you improve your communication your relationship will automatically be improved.**

Short Term Pain For Long Term Gain

How are we going to deal with real life confrontations in our marriage? **THROUGH CONFLICT RESOLUTION!** *This is going to depend on **how committed** you are to each other, **how well you communicate** with each other, and **how well you cooperate** with each other.*

"Blows that wound cleanse away evil, and strokes for correction reach to the innermost parts" (Proverbs 20:30AMP).

So come, let's make a covenant, you and I, and it will be a witness to our commitment"
(Genesis 31:44 NLT).

The Law Of Conflict Resolution

"Patient persistence pierces through indifference; gentle speech breaks down rigid defenses"
(Proverbs 25:15MSG).

Oftentimes in the process of resolving a conflict, if husband and wife would reverse the roles- see the other person's point of view, the problem they are encountering would solve itself. If each spouse would see each other's perspective, the problem would become so small until it would actually lose its value for discussion.

Anger and conflict can be linked together. To separate anger from what started the conflict, think about 'who you are' and not 'what was said'. In order to bring resolution, you and your spouse need to come to the conclusion that if my idea is not the best idea then we should let the best idea win. You and your spouse have to generate good ideas and have an open-minded willingness to listen to each other's ideas. Choose to resist the temptation to fight for your idea if it is not truly the best one. Fighting to make your idea the best one could mean you are too close to allowing anger to separate you from 'who you are', which is not what you want to happen. Ideas come from you but you don't come from your ideas. You and your spouse must have a team mentality when it comes to working together. Your spouse is not the enemy. You all are a team. Trust your spouse to know that they have your best interest at heart and desire to resolve the issue as much as you want to.

✳ We must focus on the word *'RESOLUTION'* <u>**and not on who's right, who's wrong, or who's going to win!**</u> Conflict resolution is not *'conflict insulation'*.

Conflict insulation is when you are talking to someone else who has experienced or continues to experience similar painful conflicts like your own. This false sense of 'comfort' will actually insulate the person from getting the much needed help they really need. Real conflict resolution involves listening to each other's heart and being willing to forgive.

Blow-outs And Focused Confrontation

Yes, confrontation is necessary and good. It's not however, a license to tell your spouse off. It's also not fighting with your spouse. We need confrontation because it helps us to prevent blow-outs. A 'blow-out' is a buildup of frustration, anger, hurts, and disappointments. By dealing with frustrations and anger, etc. through focused confrontation before these things build up, *you activate your relationship's pressure valve and prevent the possibility of serious damage to your marriage.* REMEMBER: IT IS THE HIDDEN DAMAGE THAT OFTEN LEADS TO A 'BLOW-OUT'. Both spouses must also never be physically, verbally, mentally, or emotionally abusive to each other. You never want to speak death to your spouse in words or actions even in the most heated of confrontations. Name calling and making false accusations in the midst of a blow-out will only lead to further damage.

> **Master communication and you will manage the conflict.**

My wife and I had a 'holy blow-out'. I kept aggravating my wife. She kept telling me to stop but I continued aggravating her until she had enough and she said, 'stop it, you nut!' Can you believe my little lady would call me a nut! This happened some 20 years ago. We always share this humorous story with other couples. We've learned throughout the years that blowouts will come but they can be repaired or mended.

Some mental marriage motivators to help you and your spouse enhance those communication skills:

1. How do you keep the communication channel open? By keeping your heart open towards each other.
2. Good relationships are built and sustained on communication.
3. Communication- without it you travel alone.
4. A good communicator takes something complex and turns it into something simple.
5. Communication is not just what you say but how you say it.
6. Effective communicators focus on the person with whom they are communicating.
7. Credibility precedes great communication.
8. A good communicator first believes in what he or she says.
9. As you communicate, never forget that the goal of all communication is action.
10. Every time you speak to your spouse give them something to feel, something to remember, and something to do.

Notes And Nuggets I Can Use For My Marriage And Personal Development:

4

Inner Healing Is Important To Your Marriage

I believe one of the most vulnerable areas that the enemy uses as an entrance into a marriage is the lack of inner healing.

Jesus said in Luke 4:18-19, "The Spirit of the LORD is upon Me, because He has anointed Me to preach the gospel to the poor; He has sent Me to heal the brokenhearted, to proclaim liberty to the captives and recovery of sight to the blind, to set at liberty those who are oppressed; to proclaim the acceptable year of the LORD."

Jesus was saying that He was anointed by the Father to bring good news to the poor, to give them hope for the state that they were in, with the knowledge that God can and will change their lives forever- not only spiritually, but also naturally, which would include our spirit, body and soul (our emotions, thoughts, and feelings). The Lord said that He is anointed to heal the brokenhearted. Oftentimes, an individual's soul has been fragmented, shattered, and traumatized. The need for inner healing is a result of pain, bitterness, unforgiveness, injustice, etc., and making inner vows. An ***inner vow*** is a type of stronghold in which a person makes a promise to him or herself as a result of a painful situation (whether physically, mentally, or emotionally).

We make common inner vows such as, 'I will never trust anyone.' The problem is that when we make such a vow like this it will hinder the growth of your marriage and cause you not to trust your spouse, or cause you to have negative thoughts about your spouse like saying, I'm going to have my own saving and checking accounts because I don't know what my spouse may do.' Or ' My spouse is always working over- I hope they aren't cheating on me.' Another common inner vow we sometimes make is 'I'm going to make it happen myself.' Now you are married and trying to do things or accomplish things independently from your husband or wife, which may not be the best decision.

We often make inner vows out of *bitter judgment*. Bitter judgment is when we make a decision, statement, or give an answer to a question but it is done out of past hurts or unforgiveness. For example, judging our parents out of bitterness we make vows and statements like,' I will never be like my father or mother.' Now you are married and a parent yourself, and have not been healed inwardly from all the bitterness you had toward your parents. This causes problems in your relationship with your husband or wife because you are dealing with your own children in their life problems worse than your mother or father dealt with you. Inner vows and bitter judgment never work. Bitterness cannot work righteousness (James 3:14), nor can it take the place of the Holy Spirit. When you are functioning out of an inner vow or bitterness, you're going to begin to make things hard on your spouse.

One of the main reasons why people can't get free from inward hurts is because of unforgiveness. Having unforgiveness in your marriage can be very challenging. If we won't forgive our brother, then God said He won't forgive us (Matthew 6:14-15) When we fail to forgive our brother we bind up what we ourselves need from heaven. When we loose our brother in forgiveness, we loose what we need from heaven (Matthew 18:18).

> *Bitterness can't work*
> *righteousness,*
> *nor can it take the place of*
> *the Holy Spirit.*

In your marriage there are things you are going to need from the Lord and you don't want unforgiveness to stop you from receiving these things. When we fail to forgive others, we place our own emotions in prison (Matthew 18:30). It will be difficult for you to express how you really feel about your spouse if there is unforgiveness in your heart. Forgive and let it go- place it in God's hand.

"Then Peter came to Him and said, "Lord, how often shall my brother sin against me, and I forgive him? Up to seven times?" Jesus said to him, "I do not say to you, up to seven times, but up to seventy times seven"
(Matthew 18:21-22).

Jesus wants us to walk and live with a forgiving heart. It must become a lifestyle because you will need to forgive each other as husband and wife as well as children or other family members as you continue to travel along life's journey.

Here is some revelation on forgiveness I believe will bless your marriage:

1. Forgiveness does not mean you shouldn't hold the person accountable for the bad choices they made.
2. Forgiveness is not healing but it is the first step for healing.
3. We must forgive all- not just those we love.

I can't share enough about the importance of receiving inner healing. I am certain that the lack of it will cause delays, hindrances, or in some cases, bring a marriage to divorce. The lack of inner healing causes your heart to become hard and very insensitive to each other. This is especially true when one or both spouses are in a situation where they need words of affirmation or encouragement but instead are showing or receiving apathy toward the problem that spouse is encountering. Inner healing requires a change of heart in order for the person to really be changed. There are so many couples that have no idea that if they receive inner healing many of their marital problems would be solved! It's because of this fact, I'm led to share this very critical information with you so that you and your spouse can improve your life personally, bring healing into your marriage, and for some, even save your marriage.

I believe King David battled with the lack of inner healing because of how his father treated him (I Samuel 16:10-13). Jesse made seven of his sons pass before Samuel to see which one would be anointed king. Samuel told Jesse that the Lord had not chosen these. Jesse didn't bring David or even mention his name until Samuel asked him were all of his sons present. Samuel knew that God hadn't made a mistake. Jesse then told him that he did, in fact, have a younger son, which Samuel then requested to bring before him.

I believe this could have affected David's life up until the time he fell into sin with Bathsheba and had her husband Uriah killed (II Samuel 11:1-27). David wrote Psalm 51. Verse 10 says 'create in me a clean heart, O God, and renew a steadfast spirit within me.' A broken heart can limit or restrict your spiritual growth until you get healed within. The word 'broken' means, 'to break into pieces, to crush and shatter' while the word 'hearted' refers to your thoughts and feelings. Jesus told us that He came to heal the brokenhearted (Luke 4:18).

The diagrams on the following pages can help explain the process of inner healing that needs to take place in the life of a husband or wife.

Inner Healing: I Need To Be Healed.

Spirit of Rejection:

Fear   Pride

1. You Must Want To Be Healed.

2. Inner Healing Is A Partnership Between You & God.

3. You Can't Be Healed Without God & God Can't Heal You Without Your Cooperation.

4. We Must Identify The Areas We Need To Be Healed In.

Yes- I Am Ready To Be Healed.

Transforming My Mind: You Must Remove All Ungodly Belief Concerning God & Yourself.

Making My Armour Strong.

Bearing Fruits: When You Are No Longer Bearing Bad Fruit But Are Bearing Good Fruit- That's When You Know You Are Healed!

5. You Must Be Wiling To Make The Sacrifices-Making Sacrifices Is The Pathway To Inner Healing.

6. Forgiveness Is The Foundation Of Inner Healing.

7. You Must War With The Word, Driving The Word Of God Into Your Spirit By Confessing It Daily.

As an individual, take some time to see what areas you need to be healed inwardly in. Then as God begins to work in you, you will be able to identify areas in your marriage that need to be healed as you get healed personally. Take some time to earnestly pray and ask God to show you specific areas that you need to be healed in. Trust Him to reveal those areas to you and let Him take you step by step through the process to break inner vows and to forgive those who have hurt you. There may be some areas that you are not aware of that will require God to reveal to you.

Your Marriage

Brokenhearted

'Broken' Means:

1. To Break Into Pieces
2. To Crush
3. To Shatter

'Hearted' Means:

- Your Thoughts and Feelings

Keys To Receive Inner Healing

1. Understanding That Inner Healing Is A Partnership Between You and God
2. Timing & Order
3. Making Sacrifices
4. Give & Receive Forgiveness
5. Repentance
6. Connecting with God
7. Connecting with Others

When A Husband Or Wife Need Inner Healing

Light Of The World

Your world should be a light (Matt. 5:14,15).

The World You Are Creating Should Be Open.

Your role as a husband or wife requires that you keep your world open to your spouse.

You may find that as you break inner vows, forgive those who have hurt you, and allow God to heal you inwardly, many problems you are experiencing in your marriage will be resolved or easier to deal with. The presence of inward pain, the need for inner healing, and the need to rid ourselves of inner vows affect our ability to have an accurate perception of people and situations. Even your perception and view of yourself will change for the better.

Take An Assessment Of Your Pain Level:

Pain Levels
(Hebrews 4:15; Colossians 3:15)

Level I

1. I can't do this now.

2. He or she knew what they did.

3. Yes, I am still angry – they didn't mean what they said when they said they were sorry.

4. Sometimes I feel bound by fear or rejection.

5. I don't see myself like that.

6. I always see the negative first, I can't help it.

Level II

1. I work well with some people.

2. I forgive them but I'm struggle with trusting them.

3. I'm expressing what I feel with the love of God.

4. I moved out from what I thought was comfortable for me and now I feel liberated in God's love.

5. Those that are close to me, said I'm better in speaking negative things than positive things.

Level III

1. I love God and His people.

2. I'm praying for the person that hurt me because I can see the pain and hurts in their life.

3. God, keep those walls down that kept you and others out.

4. It is great to be led by the Holy Spirit in relationships and in the use of my gifts.

5. I can't remember the last time I was depressed or stressed out.

Don't be afraid to allow God to show you where your pain level is at. As you continue to receive inner healing, your pain levels will go down.

40

How to get rid of inner vows:

1. Recognize the inner vow(s) that you have made.

2. Forgive the individual(s) who played any part in causing you to make the inner vow.

3. Confess and repent for making the inner vow(s).

4. Ask God to pull down the stronghold of the inner vow and then revoke its power over you.

Prayer against the spirit of rejection

Father in the name of Jesus, I worship you, with my spirit, soul and body. Father I need your help, because the spirit of rejection is hindering my marriage. I'm so insecure but Lord you have empowered me, with your spirit and I break the inner vow that opened the door of the spirit of rejection in my life. I renounce that spirit now, in the name of Jesus. I have the spirit of love and power. In Jesus' name, Amen.

Notes And Nuggets I Can Use For My Marriage And Personal Development:

5

Sex And Intimacy:
Couples Should Be Lovers In The Lord

Being a lover to each other (sexually) is based upon no one else and nothing else. Your words to your spouse should be, 'My body craves for you. I want to please you and not a fantasy.'

God gave me this profound revelation on the topic of intimacy in marriage several years ago, that having sex with your spouse is one of the most powerful experiences to have with your spouse. If helps to establish both individuals into becoming one flesh, helps war off any sexual temptation of the flesh, and helps reduce and relieve stress from the body and soul. Sex is wonderful.

God gave Apostle Paul some awesome revelation regarding sex in marriage (I Corinthians 7: 1-5). These verses explain how spouses don't own their bodies but they own each other's bodies. Paul stated that they should have sex with each other when asked. That doesn't mean to be selfish or not considerate of each other's personal state or condition each other may be in during the request for sexual intercourse.

The Apostle Paul mentioned that fasting and prayer should be a part of your marriage. I believe that fasting and prayer, helps keep the intimacy in the marriage beautiful and healthy but he cautious those that are married to fast and pray, but (come together again). He was talking about sex.

You Should Never Have A Third Partner In Your Bedroom.

We all know how sexual our culture is today. As married couples we must value the gift of sex God gave us to enjoy within the confines of our marriage. We must fight on a daily basis anything the enemy will try to use to defile, undermine, or devalue our sexual relationship. As a couple you must keep the enemy of sexual lust out of your bedroom.

"...He who commits adultery destroys his own soul.."
(Prov. 6:32).

"Stolen water is sweet" (Prov. 9:17a).

Lust steals the passion and intimacy from your marriage. Stolen water is sweet but your own water is better.

How do you keep this enemy of sexual lust out? You have to keep these three doors closed from this spirit:
1. The ears
2. The eyes
3. The mouth

To overcome the spirit of lust you must grow in the love God has for you and in the love you have for each other. This kind of love causes the door to be open in the area of communication. Whatever or whoever you love will always bring enjoyment in talking or being with them to you. Love, communication, and accountability will help you defeat this enemy to your marriage.

Your body belongs to your spouse and his or her body belongs to you (I Corinthians 7:4).

"Now as to the matters of which you wrote me. It is well [and by that I mean advantageous, expedient, profitable, and wholesome] for a man not to touch a woman [to cohabit with her] but to remain unmarried. But because of the temptation to impurity and to avoid immortality, let each [man] have his own wife and let each [woman] have her own husband. The husband should give to his wife her conjugal right (goodwill, kindness, and what is due her as his wife), and likewise the wife to her husband. For the wife does not have [exclusive] authority and control over her own body, but the husband [has his right]; likewise also the husband does not have [exclusive] authority and control over his body, but the wife [has her rights]. Do not refuse and deprive and defraud each other [of our due marital rights], except perhaps by mutual consent for a time, so that you may devote yourselves unhindered to prayer. But afterwards resume martial relations, lest Satan tempt you [to sin] through your lack of restraint of sexual desire."
(I Corinthians 7:1-5 AMP)

One of the hot questions concerning sex in a marriage for some couples is, 'is oral sex right or wrong within our marriage?' I believe when the scripture says, *"Marriage is honorable among all, and the bed undefiled; but fornicators and adulterers God will judge" (Hebrews 13:4),* that the word 'undefiled' means to make clean or pure. In essence, whatever method, positions, perfumes, oils, etc. a husband and wife choose to incorporate into their sexual relationship with each other can fall under the category of being 'undefiled' if it is pleasing to God and to each other. There also needs to be agreement between both spouses that they are willing to do what is requested by their spouse. I believe that if one is forced to do something that is uncomfortable for them it will not please God or the other spouse. Love is always the basis for what we do in our marriage.

I believe that sex should always be joyful and pleasing to both spouses. Good hygiene plays a role in the sexual relationship in a marriage as well. Timing and foreplay is essential in a good sex life. Pornographic materials are never needed.

If there is some type of sickness that prevents actual vaginal penetration during sexual activity, husbands and wives should know that penetration is only a part of a great sex life. To embrace each other in the nude and to lavish each other with intimate touches and kisses are great as well. Praying that God can bring healing in that aspect of your intimacy is a good thing to do. Never stop trying to please each other sexually.

Sex is important in a marriage but marriage is not built on sex, nor does sex keep a marriage. Sex doesn't give marriage happiness or lasting joy. Sex doesn't keep the fire kindled in a marriage. Sex can't keep you missing each other when you're not in each other's presence. It doesn't have the depth to keep the marriage during challenging times. The genuine closeness and intimacy you have in your relationship will make all the difference.

The most important components that keep a marriage strong, healthy and exciting for life is love for God, and love, commitment, and friendship both spouses have for each other. Even during the golden years of marriage, when both are not as sexually active, to hold each other in their arms, will be just as powerful as sex. To be with each other on a sunny day or on a rainy night will bring and give both spouses joy unspeakable. Joy, love, commitment, faithfulness, and love for God is what's keeping my marriage of 37 years. I would be remiss if I didn't tell you what Jesus said about sex. I think you can also relate this to sex in marriage- Matthew 5:28. Jesus said if you look on a woman or man to lust, you have already had sex in your heart (paraphrased). Thus, the husband and wife can look at each other, being nude or clothed, not engaging in intercourse, and still enjoy each other. Wow, that is powerful! Thank you Jesus, you know how to keep the fun in a marriage. Jesus has a bride- the Church is Jesus' Bride (Revelation 19:7). His love for us gives us the greatest example of how to love and cherish our mates, just as Christ lavishes His people (the Church) with love.

Keep your communication going and keep your heart open to each other- this will keep the passion and intimacy going and growing.

> *Being a lover to each other*
> *sexually is based upon*
> *no one else and nothing else.*

Notes And Nuggets I Can Use For My Marriage And Personal Development:

6

Where Is Your Marriage?

If you are married and doing well: You are in I Corinthians 7:5:

"So don't refuse sex to each other, unless you agree not to have sex for a little while, in order to spend time in prayer. Then Satan won't be able to tempt you because of your lack of self-control".

This is a good time in your marriage to make it better. You can continue attending marriage retreats or couples' getaways to keep you informed and help keep your marriage healthy and joyful. The added benefit is that you and your spouse will be a great help to others who need a couple like the two of you in their lives. Your marriage is strong enough to bear the burden of another couple's marriage that needs love, patience, wisdom, and revelation. This is why it's vital that when your marriage is doing well you need to keep a hedge of righteousness around it. By this I mean more Godly wisdom from others, and most of all, keeping God as the first person in your life. You always want to keep building your marriage because marriage is not for a season or time, but for life.

If you are married but are unhappy: The first person in your life must be God. I know this may sound like it's too simple to be true, but I'm writing from experience. God is the answer- Him alone with His son Jesus, and

His Spirit (the Holy Spirit). The Holy Spirit can help you walk through difficult times in your marriage. He will give you the joy in the midst of challenges you face. He won't become your spouse because that's not his role, but He can help you with wisdom on how to make your marriage better, without losing all hope. I promise you, you can be unhappy in your marriage, almost at your last stand, but if you begin to intercede for your relationship, without allowing it to be your main focus but have God as the main focus, your prayers will become more effective. I do realize this is not easy but you will have peace and joy in Christ (James 5:16-18). To say prayer works is an understatement!

If you are married but separated where do you start? You should start in I Corinthians 7:11:

"But even if she does depart, let her remain unmarried or be reconciled to her husband. And a husband is not to divorce his wife."

The first thing you shouldn't do is start seeing someone else. Please don't do that- this would be a HUGE mistake. You should focus on your marriage and not on pleasing your soul. When you get involved with someone else, you have now created another problem- *__an ungodly soul-tie.__* This is not the answer. **It might please the flesh, but will damage you and your marriage.**

The wife should work on being friendly again. She should pray and talk to God concerning being her husband's friend again. She should work on allowing God to prepare her to receive that which the devil took from their friendship. She should be willing to allow God to use her husband to restore that which the devil has taken. She should work on leaving the past in the past.

The Husband should work on getting his wife to become closer. He should show her what his covering is made of. His covering should be made up of...

- 40% "I love you!" Christ's Way
- 40% "You can trust me!"
- 5% "I do hear you!"
- 5% "I will open up!"
- 5% "I am romantic!"
- 5% "I miss you!"

This is not a perfect solution to the problem of separation, but I believe it is a great start. Most of the time, when couples separate, they do not know where to start. They will waste time, money and in some cases cause the marriage to become irreconcilable. I believe the Holy Spirit (The Helper) is always ready to help us win in any life issues, if we are willing to trust His decision with our whole heart. *"Trust in the LORD with all your heart, and lean not on your own understanding; in all your ways acknowledge Him, and He shall direct your paths" (Prov. 3:5-6).*

If you are married but you were separated and are now reconciling: You should start in Ephesians 5:21: "Submitting yourselves one to another in the fear of God." Husband and wife should work on being humble towards God with a greater respect for who He is and because He is God!

In addition, both spouses should try hard ***to keep the past in the past***. Don't allow the memories of the flesh, to tempt you to talk about the reasons why the separation started or who was at fault when God repairs some areas of your marriage, or when He begins to restore your marriage in its entirety. Don't allow Satan to come back with backlash and steal what God has restored. I have learned over the years that in any of life's problems, prayer with supplication is the key. The word 'supplication' means, 'extended prayer'. I believe it means to pray some more until whatever you are asking for has been received, or to pray until you have peace about the problem. *"Do not be anxious about anything, but in every situation, by prayer and petition, with thanksgiving, present your requests to God. And the peace of God, which transcends all understanding, will guard your hearts and your minds in Christ Jesus"* (Philippians 4:6-7NIV). The husband and the wife should work on being humble towards each other with kind and gentle words. Kind and gentle words can break the back of a "flesh attack!"

Your Spouse Is Unsaved Or Lukewarm

If your husband or wife is not saved or has no walk with God or one that's not very strong, find out what your he or she likes to do outside of sin and support them with your heart. Don't allow your mouth to interfere. If you have decided to stay in the marriage then stop worrying and seek God for the divine purpose of the marriage. Every marriage has a divine purpose that will drive that marriage closer to God and to each other. If you seek God He will give you strategies that will help you to out maneuver over the enemy.

Two key principals that we must incorporate into our marriage are the power of leadership and the power of submission. Every husband has an anointing to lead his wife and family. It takes Jesus in the husband's life for that anointing to be fully activated. Every wife has an anointing to help her husband and it takes Jesus in her life to activate this anointing. In order to keep this anointing flowing within the marriage, make a great effort to totally eliminate name-calling, fighting, lying, and being unfaithful.

The Spirit Of A Scoffer Is A Threat To Any Marriage

A scoffer – one that doesn't take anything that's Godly seriously.

A scoffer has no power because there has been no application of wisdom and knowledge to bring any change within them. The scoffer spirit doesn't have concern for the marriage but actually comes against the marriage.

There is a difference in being concerned and coming against your marriage. Being concerned is designed to see improvement. When you are concerned you are asking the question. "What can I do to help?" It is also taking the third person (self) out of your marriage and keeping the first person (Jesus) in your marriage. Being concerned means treating your marriage as a Godly institution.

In a marriage there is middle management. This is the concept of headship and the power of delegated authority flowing in your marriage. Spouses must first come under authority before they can lead in their home and not vice-versa. In addition, there needs to be conflict management in the marriage. This is the communication, cooperation, and compromise within the relationship. And remember, don't cut into each other's souls. Cutting into your spouse's soul is when you speak words or do something that would bring them deep pain to their soul, which entails their heart, mind, and emotions. Soul repair is very costly and can bring great damage to your relationship.

Coming against your marriage is designed to stop improvement. Coming against your marriage is saying, "I'm not doing anything until I get ready" or "I'm doing enough. When both spouses have agreed to stay together and "to dwell" the elements that need to be expressed regularly with the mind of being concerned for your marriage are compliments, compassion, and comfort.

What category does your marriage fit in?
a. Both spouses were unsaved when they got married.
b. Both spouses were saved when they got married.
c. One spouse was saved but married someone that wasn't but told everyone that the individual was saved.
d. Both spouses were saved but didn't wait on God to lead them into marriage and married out of sexual lust. (Note: Lust consists of greed – an uncontrollable desire for something, wanting too much to please one's self and selfishness – caring very little about anyone else and a whole lot about oneself.)

What Do You Do When Your Spouse Does Not Want To Cooperate Or Is Under The Influence of satan?
You must practice *kingdom intercession.* Kingdom intercession consists of seven things:
1. Ownership (I Corinthians 7:4)
2. Identification (Identify the enemy.) (Ephesians 6:12)
3. Intercession (Stand in the gap.) (I Timothy 2:1)
4. Warring with the word (Working in the flesh won't work.) (Hebrews 4:12)
5. Corporate prayer (I need some back up.) (Deuteronomy 32:30; Leviticus 26:8; Matthew 18:19-20)
6. Corporate fasting (I need some help to break through.) (Isaiah 58:6)
7. Self-examination (Stay blameless.) (Psalm 139:23; Jeremiah 17:10; I Peter 3:1)

Remember, in order for your marriage to grow there must be some denying and dying. The fastest way for your flesh to die in a marriage is application and appreciation.

Prayer for Forgiveness

Father in the name of Jesus, through the blood of Jesus, we worship you. We ask you to help us to forgive each other, so that we can move forward and love you and love each other. We ask you to help us to quiet our souls and forgive from our heart. In Jesus' Name, Amen.

> **Don't cut into each other's soul-soul repair is very costly in a marriage.**

Notes And Nuggets I Can Use For My Marriage And Personal Development:

7

Making My Marriage Better

Marriage Is Better Than Sex – But Sex Is More Popular

A marriage has to be built. What are the elements to build a marriage? What constitutes or makes a marriage? Does sex enhance a marriage spiritually so? Sex is important to marriage but doesn't have anything to do with building a marriage.

The elements that build a marriage are...

Trust, Commitment, and Communication

All these elements are tied into love. These are more powerful than sex! Trust, commitment, and communication are all tied into love. You may desire sex more than the elements (trust, commitment, and communication, etc) but that doesn't mean that sex is more powerful; just more popular.

Marriage is not for a season or time, but for life.

I feel led to pray right now, I believe these words are anointed. Join me in this prayer: *Father in the name of Jesus, help my marriage. Let it be built upon your love and not on what I may think or desire, in the name of Jesus. I will trust you. Amen.*

Making Your Marriage Better Is Up To You!

How do you make your marriage better?   You start off with a desire. You must know the purpose of your marriage (divine and human) and who's controlling your marriage. You must be able to accept each other for who you are. You and your spouse must be best friends. Friendship is built upon trust and acceptance. You should never have a friend that is closer to you than your spouse is!

<u>*Trust*</u> – to believe in; confide in; count on; esteem; depend upon; expect help from, etc.

<u>*Acceptance*</u> – approval; surrender; endure, allow; receive; suffer, etc.

As you commit to a great friendship express these words to your mate:

It is between you and I, and we won't tell anyone else. You are my best friend. You made me feel good opening up to you. I am sorry, please forgive me for any hurts or pain I've caused, because I don't want to lose my friendship with you. I don't ever want to miss talking and being with you. I understand your weaknesses and I want to help you because you are my best friend. Your weakness is going to help me become stronger and my weakness is going to help you become stronger. Why? Because we are friends!

Who's The Law Around Here? Three Outlaws That Are An Enemy To Your Marriage

The most unwanted outlaw of a marriage is the *spirit of pride*. Pride is self justifiable, arrogant behavior (stuck on self). It is my way, my thought, my money, and my righteousness most of the time (Proverbs 11:2; 13:10; 14:3; 16:18; 29:23; I Peter 5:5). The very meaning of this word makes it so bad! The only way to defeat pride is with submission (Ephesians 5:22; I Peter 5:5-6). Submission must form a "posse" with humility, gentleness, patience, and forbearance. All four of these elements will get their authority from submission.

> *Never place in-laws, children, or any other family members before your spouse.*

The second outlaw to a marriage is the outlaw of unfaithfulness. This is when one or both spouses are not in observance of the vows they have taken. Unfaithfulness can also be giving in to evil words such as flirtatious flattery and lying, and the giving of your body to evil deeds such as sexual intercourse with someone other than your spouse or pornography (Genesis 6:5; Proverbs 12:20; 6:24, 26, 32; I Corinthians 6:18-20; 7:4). In order to defeat the outlaw of unfaithfulness you must have sacrificial love for your spouse. Ephesians 5:28 states, *"So husbands ought to love their own wives as their own bodies; he who loves his wife loves himself."* You have to love your husband or wife so much that you are willing to sacrifice your flesh on the altar of "touch not, handle not, and have not".

The third unwanted outlaw is the outlaw of unmanaged finances. Unmanaged finances means your financial state of affairs is in such bad shape that you are stealing from God, your kids and your creditors because your finances are being poorly managed or not managed at all (Malachi 3:8; Proverbs 13:22; 19:14; II Kings 4:7; Matthew 18:30). To manage your finances both spouses may need help. The spouse that handles and manages the finances better should be the one to take care of the finances of your home. Don't leave or resign from jobs without much prayer. Have a good work ethic on your job. Stay and spend within your means! Be open to financial counsel if you and your spouse know it will be beneficial to helping you get your finances in order or on track. Never lend or give out large sums of money without your spouse's knowledge and consent.

Keep these areas managed and keep your marriage enjoyable:
- o Managing your finances
- o Staying in good health
- o Disciplining your children
- o Sex
- o Making good decisions

There are several areas satan desires to attack in our marriages but we must know what God is saying concerning our marriage, not being ignorant of the enemy's devices (Ephesians 5:17; II Corinthians 2:11).

There are some areas in our marriage that take the wisdom and revelation for God to work through in order to experience breakthrough in the spouse's life personally and cause the marriage to be healthy in every area: We refer to these areas as 'God Jobs' because they are areas deep within us that will take the power of God, prayer and a commitment to keep loving your spouse until they receive the inner healing and total breakthrough needed oftentimes from their past:

Baggage We Bring Into Our Marriages And A Job That Only God Can Do (God Jobs):

1. Provide inner healing from mental and emotional pain
2. Help us break inner vows
3. Help us bring closure to unresolved internal issues
4. Heal us from past hurts
5. Heal us from childhood issues
6. Heal us from any type of dysfunction
7. Heal us from the pain of an untimely death of spouse or loved one

These charts below can help you and your spouse identify what the enemy can use to bring damage or even destroy your relationship:

These 5 areas can create major problems if not dealt with using wisdom from God:

5 Things That Can Release Toxic Fumes Into Your Marriage:

⚠ CAUTION
LAZINESS

DANGER
Blow-Outs

DO NOT
Flirtation
ENTER

WARNING
Empty
Love Tank

Be Careful
Body Odor

Be committed to make every effort to improve these areas if you know they are a hindrance to your relationship with your mate. Let God give you a strategy or plan to eliminate any of these areas that can be very problematic or cause your marriage to be on its way to the grave if the issues are not addressed.

Below are 5 major areas that can potentially destroy a marriage:

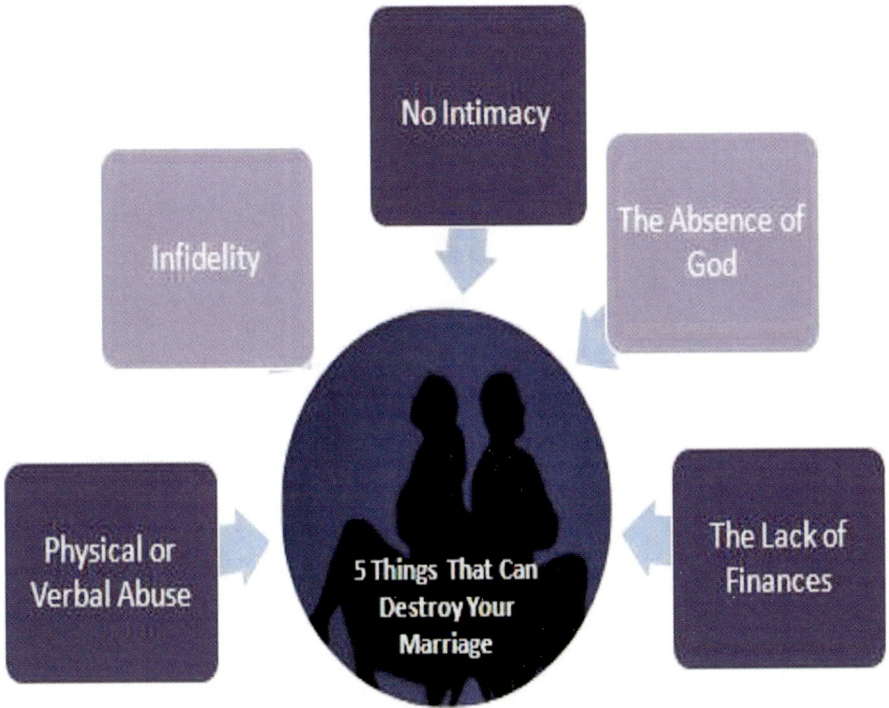

No Intimacy

Infidelity

The Absence of God

Physical or Verbal Abuse

5 Things That Can Destroy Your Marriage

The Lack of Finances

If you are experiencing issues in any of these areas, make an effort to seek out Godly counsel to help you. If you have a desire to see your marriage work, pray and ask God to help you or you and your mate together kill anything that is trying to kill your marriage. You cannot do it alone.

Helpful marriage motivators you can incorporate into your marriage:

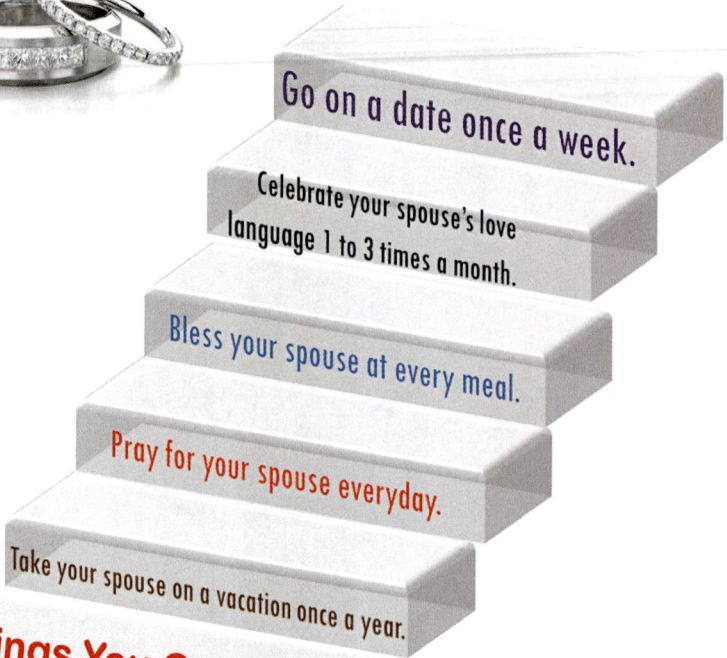

Go on a date once a week.

Celebrate your spouse's love language 1 to 3 times a month.

Bless your spouse at every meal.

Pray for your spouse everyday.

Take your spouse on a vacation once a year.

5 Things You Can Do To Make A Good Marriage Better:

Gary Chapman's book, The Five Love Languages: How to Express Heartfelt Commitment to Your Mate, is a great tool to use in discovering your love language and your spouse's love language.

Prayer for Wealth

Father we honor you and worship you with our hearts. You have given us power to get wealth. Help us in Jesus' name, to manage our money well and be good stewards. We ask you to forgive us for not managing your money right. We place your money back in your hand. Show us and teach us how to manage your money and we ask you to bless us with more for your glory. In Jesus' name, Amen.

Prayer for Healing

Father we worship you in spirit and truth. You are our God and we love you. This sickness has no power over us. Because Isaiah 53:1 says, 'Who has believed our report? And to whom has the arm of the Lord been revealed? We believe your report. By your Son's stripes we are healed. We will walk in our healing; we command our bodies to come into agreement with your word, Father. In Jesus name, Amen.

Making My Marriage Better Assessment

Use the information below to identify where your relationship is with your spouse:

How Full Is Your Couple's Cup?
*(You Want Your Cup Full
And Running Over- Psalm 23:5d)*

Your relationship is like a cup; its an open vessel that has the capacity to hold , receive and pour out things (love, feelings, desires, thoughts, words, affection, etc.) at varied degrees (different stages of your marriage) .

Your cup is full-
Your marriage is sound, stable, growing healthy. Each spouse is getting what they need from God and each other.

Your cup is empty-
Warning! If you want to save your marriage it needs to be a priority. One or both spouses are lacking what they need from God and each other in many areas.

Your cup is half-full-
Your marriage is somewhat healthy but there are some areas that one or both spouses are lacking in as far as what they need from God and each other. Your marriage needs more attention right away.

Don't be afraid to seek God for what your marriage needs! This is one of the greatest investments you can make for the benefit of you and your spouse. Give your marriage what it really needs and you and your mate will be fulfilled. *Remember: "Marriage is like having sex – if you want it to continue to be good then both of you should work very hard at pleasing each other.*

Here are some signs of a healthy marriage, one on its way to the grave, and a dead one that you can use to evaluate your own marriage. See if any of these apply to your marriage:

Signs of a healthy marriage-
- The marriage has a God-given purpose
- Has been tested and tempted and is still standing strong
- Has had some ups and downs but each spouse still enjoys spending time with each other
- Have had some disagreements and arguments but were able to forgive each other and keep moving forward
- When both spouses have agreed to never verbally, physically, or mentally abuse each other
- Enjoy each other sexually
- Enjoy looking at each other
- Communication is healthy- each spouse listens as well as talks to each other

Signs of a marriage on its way to the grave-
- When the communication becomes arguing, fussing, and complaining most of the time
- When communication is suppressed or kept within concerning how one spouse feels
- When communication is not about planning, investing, building, vacation, or how you feel about one another
- There is no strong desire to be intimate with each other
- When there's nothing to talk about

- When there's nothing to do but work and go home
- When one or both of you are functioning out of a hurt soul (need inner healing) that hasn't been healed properly

Signs of a marriage that is dead-
- There is no God-given purpose for the marriage
- No healthy communication
- No sex life
- Unfaithfulness
- No desire to get help or make the marriage better

Which of the following is hurting my marriage? (Check all that apply)

1. Lack of communication

2. Not spending enough time together

3. Lack of honesty

4. Not being open enough

5. One of us doesn't enjoy sex or not enough sex

6. Not enough finances

7. Unfaithfulness

8. Too much negative criticism

9. Lack of prayer and the word of God

10. The past

11. Lack of trust

12. In-Laws

13. Children

Which of the following can make my marriage better: (check all that apply)

1. I will stop putting off what I can do right now for tomorrow.
2. I need to stop being so critical.
3. I need to start praying more fervently.
4. I need to spend more time with God and less time watching television.
5. I need my spouse to feel good about me.
6. I need to trust God and my spouse more by:
    a. Being more open.
    b. Start to listen to God more and not the devil.
7. I need to start spending more time and money on my spouse.
8. I need to show my spouse that I have faith in God by:
    a. Being willing to make changes and not stay the same.
    b. Not being so tight with money.
    c. Not spending so carelessly.
    d. Not spending so much on my relatives.
9. I need to stop being selfish by pleasing my spouse first before I please myself in all areas.

Here Are Some Specific Things We Need To Focus On In Our Marriage:

The following pages display our marriage life resume that my wife and I created. What do I mean by 'marriage life resume'? I'd like to share with you the divine purpose God gave my wife and I for our own marriage.

God gave Adam a divine assignment (Genesis 2:15). *"Then the Lord God took the man and put him in the garden of Eden to tend and keep it."* God then gave Adam a wife to help him with that divine assignment (Genesis 2:22). *"Then the rib which the Lord God had taken from man He made into a woman, and He brought her to the man."* I believe the divine assignment or the purpose that God has given my wife and I has helped our marriage tremendously throughout the years. I remember so many times when the devil tried to come into our marriage. We were so focused on our purpose in life for God, which kept us praying and trying to make sure that we were pleasing God. I know that helped our marriage because it brought us closer together.

This life resume is all about purpose and a process that God took us through. We got married at a young age- I was 21 and my wife was 22 years old. Within six months of our marriage we both received Christ into our lives and gave our lives to God. We wanted to share some of the life experiences we encountered as a couple as we've gone along through our purpose and process. As a couple you want to embrace and try to understand your own process. The process is what gets you from point A to point B, as a saved couple while you experience life issues and situations with thanksgiving, all while trying very hard not to complain. The bible tells us, "In everything give thanks; for this is the will of God in Christ Jesus for you" (I Thessalonians 5:18).

I realize it's easier said than done, but that's the purpose of having the Holy Spirit in our lives. He is our helper. Worship is much more productive than complaining. I pray that this life resume helps give you some understanding and blesses your marriage.

"Marriage Has A Divine Purpose"

Benny & Gerry Dozier's Life Resume
37 Years Of Marriage

1975-1980

- Benny and Gerry got saved and spirit-filled at the same time in 1976
- 2 sons were born
- Benny called to preach
- Both helped plant a church
- Both working full-time

The strengths/positive:

- Benny made a vow to stay saved & faithful to his wife
- Gerry made a vow the she wouldn't let the enemy use her to cause shame or hurt to her husband
- Benny met his spiritual father, Elder Leo & began to get counsel & wisdom
- Very good communication- a lot of talking as a couple
- Benny spent a lot of time in prayer & praying in tongues

The challenges/things that were lacking:

- Debt
- Rejection
- Fear
- Low self-esteem

1980-1985

- Bought 1st home- debt decreased
- Both active in a good, sound ministry
- Benny called to pastor in 1985
- Both received job promotions

The strengths/positive:

- The commitment toward God and each other
- Communication and cooperating, with each other, trying to make it work

The challenges/things that were lacking:

- Benny had made inner vow-not to be like his father, creating a fear of failure
- Gerry had made an inner vow- to always have her own

1985-1990

- Pastoring 9 years and very focused on ministry
- Once a week always had family time with kids and spouse

The strengths/positive:
- What kept marriage growing was our commitment to God and each other

Challenges/things that were lacking:
- Still needed inner healing
- Discussed ministry a lot but not enough about themselves

1990-1995

- The pressure of ministry (people leaving, dealing with the challenges of ministry, etc.)
- Both left their jobs, Benny of 21 years and Gerry of 23 years (God provided)

Challenges/things that were lacking:

- Didn't know how to communicate feelings to the wife concerning all that was taking place

The strengths/positive:

- A greater level of trust developed during this time.
- A greater level of communication developed. Benny began to share with his wife what areas he was being hurt in and she was able to give words of affirmation
- Both spouses getting more inner healing because of the commitment toward God & each other

1995-2000

- Benny called and commissioned to the office of an apostle
- Gerry called and commissioned to the office of a pastor and became the resident pastor of the church in Gary, Indiana

The strengths/positive:

- More solid and sound in ministry
- Communication growing better in times of heated discussion

Challenges/things that were lacking:

- Getting adjusted to the new changes taking place as taking on the office of apostle and resident pastor
- Getting adjusted to doing ministry work in two states and apart from each other

2000-2005

- Learning themselves more as individuals spiritually and naturally, which helped them to accept each other and have more empathy towards one another
- Started several businesses

Challenges/things that were lacking:

- Wife lost two loved ones in short period of time

2005-2010

- The greatest years yet-handled the most challenging situations in personal life and in ministry
- Both spouses have been able to use both gifts given by God: Wife- the gift of discernment (knowing what to fight against) and husband-leadership (how to build)
- The ministry established its first elementary school
- Gerry became the C.O.O. of the daycare center they opened several years earlier

2011-2012

- The ministry in Gary that Gerry pastors established a second elementary school and named her as the school's C.E.O.
- Years of great transition personally and in ministry
- Assignments are changing for both spouses as it relates to ministry
- International travel is among the new changes for both spouses

The strengths/positive:

- Marriage is strong enough for both spouses to be apart for periods of time
- The marriage is built to handle this season of travel domestically and internationally

Challenges/things that are lacking:

- The adjustment of not being together as much as they had been for the first 25 years of marriage
- Getting used to doing more ministry work apart from one another and abroad

Create Your Own Life Resume For You And Your Spouse:

PRAYER FOR HUSBANDS TO CONFESS

Father, in the name of Jesus, I take Your Word and confess this day that I hearken to Your wisdom. My wife and I dwell securely in confident trust, and we are without fear or dread of evil. I make my ears attentive to skillful and godly wisdom, inclining and directing my heart and mind to understanding. I apply all of my power to the quest of wisdom and understanding.

I let not mercy, kindness and truth forsake me. I bind them about my neck and write them on the tablet of my heart. I prize the wisdom of God highly and exalt her. She will exalt and promote me, bringing me honor because I embrace her. For You, Lord, are my confidence, firm and strong, and You keep my foot from being caught in a trap or hidden danger.

Where I go, the Word of God shall lead me. When I sleep, it shall keep me. When I awaken, it shall talk to me. Therefore, I will speak excellent and princely things. And the opening of my lips shall be for right things. All the words of my mouth are righteous – upright and in right standing with God – and there is nothing contrary to truth or crooked in them.

I live considerately with my wife, with an intelligent recognition of our marriage relationship. I honor my wife as physically the weaker. However, I realize that we are joint-heirs to the throne with Jesus spiritually. I do this in order that our prayers will not be hindered or cut off.

I confess that my wife and I are of one and the same mind, united in spirit, compassionate and courteous, tenderhearted and humble minded. I believe for our welfare, happiness, and protection, because we love and respect each other.

Father, I confess that we are a couple of good report, that we are successful in everything we set our hands to. We are uncompromisingly righteous. We capture human lives for You as fishers of men. As we do this, we are confident that You are the Lord God who teaches us to profit and leads us in the way we should go. We are abundantly supplied, with every need met, in the name of Jesus. We have obtained the favor of the Lord, and the will of God is done in our lives and in our children's lives.

Scripture References:
Proverbs 1:33
Proverbs 3:3
Proverbs 3:26
Proverbs 8:6, 8
Proverbs 11: 30
Proverbs 2:2
Proverbs 4:8
Proverbs 6:22
I Peter 3:7-9
Isaiah 48:17

PRAYER FOR WIVES TO CONFESS

Father, in the name of Jesus, I take Your Word and speak it out of my mouth and say that I have faith that I am a capable, intelligent, patient, and virtuous woman. I am far more precious than jewels. My value to my husband and family is far above rubies and pearls.

The heart of my husband trusts in me confidently and relies on and believes in me completely, so that he has no lack of honest gain or need of dishonest spoil.

Father, I will comfort, encourage, and do him only good as long as there is life within me. I gird myself with strength – spiritual, mental, and physical fitness for my God-given task. I taste and see that my gain from work with and for God is good. My lamp goes not out. It burns on continually through the night of any trouble, privation, or sorrow, and it warns away fear, doubt, and distrust.

I open my hand to the poor. I reach out my filled hands to the needy – whether in spirit, soul, or body. My husband is known as a success in everything he puts his hand to. Strength and dignity are my clothing, and my position in my household is strong. I am secure and at peace in knowing that my family is in readiness for the future.

I open my mouth with skillful and Godly wisdom, and in my tongue is the law of kindness and love. I look well to how things go in my household. The bread of idleness, gossip, discontent, and self-pity I will not eat.

My children rise up and call me blessed and happy. My husband boasts of and praises me, saying that I excel in all that I set my hand to. I am a woman who reverently and worshipfully loves You, Lord, and You shall give me the fruits of my hands. My works will praise me wherever I go, for Father, I confess that I am a submitted wife – simply because I want to be and I recognize Your authority. I thank You for my husband who is head over me, but who has given me (through the chain of command) the necessary power to do what Your Word says for me to do from Proverbs 31:10-31. I am as this woman is – a loving, successful, submitted wife – in the name of Jesus.

<u>Scripture Reference:</u>
Proverbs 31:10-31 (AMP)

Create a list of requests and areas to pray about daily for your marriage:

Reference Information:

The Five Love Languages: How To Express Heartfelt Commitment To Your Mate, Gary D. Chapman. Published by Northfield Publishing, 1992

Merriam-Webster Dictionary©2012 Merriam-Webster, Inc.

Contact Information

For prayer requests, speaking engagement requests or additional copies of the book you may visit our website www.powerandlightchurch.org or contact Power and Light Evangelistic Church at 708-331-9834.

If you feel there's no hope for your marriage or it's dead, God can still restore it! If you are sincere about getting the help your marriage needs send me an email at apostledozier@powerandlightchurch.org or call the church office number above for assistance.

Lydia R. Rowe

April R. Rowe

Apostle Benny L. Dozier

April R. Rowe

Rashaad Rowe